THE HAYTOR GRANITE TRAMWAY AND STOVER CANAL

A guide to retracing the route of
Dartmoor's granite from quarry to sea

HELEN HARRIS

Helen Harris .

With illustrations by George Thurlow

**Peninsula
Press**

By the same author

The Industrial Archaeology of Dartmoor
The Industrial Archaeology of the Peak District
The Bude Canal (with Monica Ellis)
The Grand Western Canal

Published by Peninsula Press Ltd
P.O. Box 31
Newton Abbot
Devon TQ12 5XH
Tel: 0803 875875

Printed in England by
The Cromwell Press, Melksham, Wiltshire.

ISBN 1 872640 28 1

CONTENTS

Winch -
Haytor Quarry

Haytor Rocks

CHAPTER ONE

The source, and the demand

Anyone who travels along the moorland road between Haytor Vale and Widecombe can hardly fail to be impressed by the breadth and wildness of the undulating scene. Granite outcrops rise dramatically from the greenness, dominated by the majestic divided mass of Hay Tor itself. At an altitude of 1,490ft this is by no means the highest of Dartmoor's tors, but it is one of the most imposing, with rockfaces that portray the hard, strong character of the material on which Dartmoor is based.

Granite, or moorstone as it was earlier known, resulted from igneous activity that occured around 290 million years ago, when molten granite from below the earth's surface forced its way upwards, forming a huge hump. Cooling slowly under pressure, the granite hardened and crystallised. During succeeding ages weathering caused erosion and gradual removal of the overlying rocks, whose nature had been altered by the great heat, exposing the granite and laying bare rugged tor formations on many of the hills.

The character and colour of the granite varies in different parts of the moor. Its main constituents are quartz, which looks like greyish glass; mica, which is usually black; and felspar, whose crystals often appear as creamy angular plates. The summit rocks of Hay Tor, like those of many of the tors, are of coarse grain, but that of the surrounding down is much finer, and recognised for its qualities of hardness and durability.

For centuries, from pre-historic times, tumbled moorstone or 'clitter' has been used by man for building and for a variety of purposes. The early dwellers found plenty of stone lying around, and removing it for their huts and walls had the added advantage of clearing areas of ground for farming activities. Later, stone taken for their own use became one of the established perquisites of those with common rights. It was generally not until the early part of the nineteenth century, however, when new techniques of cutting had been developed and demand was created by construction in towns, that quarrying from the actual bedrock was initiated.

The known value of Haytor granite made this an attractive area to exploit for building material. Already, since the 1730s, a product of granite decomposition - pipe or ball clay - was being extracted commercially a few miles down off the moor in the Bovey valley, where it had been washed from the high ground by the early erosive forces. For many years this clay was carried away by packhorses or carts along narrow lanes, and shipped from Newton Abbot down the River Teign to coastal routes. But from 1792 an improved form of transport came into being with the construction of the Stover Canal, from Newton up to Ventiford, by James Templer. His father - also called James - had purchased the 80,000 acre Stover estate, which included poor heathland in the Bovey basin and the rocks at Hay Tor, in 1765, and stone laboriously brought by horse and cart from the tor was used for his new Stover House, built before he died in 1792.

It was the Templer of the next generation, George (son of the second James, whom he succeeded in the estate in 1813) who developed Haytor Quarries commercially. Calls for good building material were coming from farther afield, notably London, particularly for use in the construction of the new London Bridge (opened in 1825), and it was probably as the result of obtaining contracts for this and other work that from about 1819 George Templer opened quarries on Haytor Down. But before dispatch of the required volume of granite could be achieved the problem of transport had to be overcome. At the lower level there was the canal, which had been in use for nearly thirty years, but from Haytor Down a fall of about 1,300ft over seven miles had to be negotiated to the waterside. Some idea of the difficulties can be gained by viewing the panorama south from Hay Tor to the distant sea and the Teign estuary, and considering the intervening descent and hilly country.

The solution was seen to lie in the construction of a tramway - an innovation, since no railway existed in Devon at that time. As iron for rails was not readily available in this remoteness from any iron-works, it was decided that the track should be formed from blocks of granite, suitably cut to carry the wheels of the horse drawn waggons. So it was that the system was laid to serve the main quarry and various smaller ones, and to carry the 'trains' down to the canal.

Opened in 1820, the tramway was in use until the late 1850s, by which time it, and the canal, had long been sold to the Duke of Somerset. The canal, reduced in length, railway-owned and leased to a clay company, continued in dwindling service into the present century. Remains of both can be traced by followers of the walking route known as the Templer Way

The first Haytor village. From an original print by T.H.Williams, dated 1829. Reproduced by kind permission of the owner, Mr J.V.Somers Cocks.

The Haytor Granite Tramway and Stover Canal

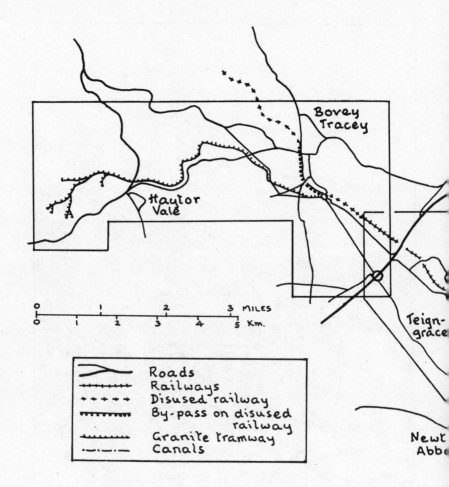

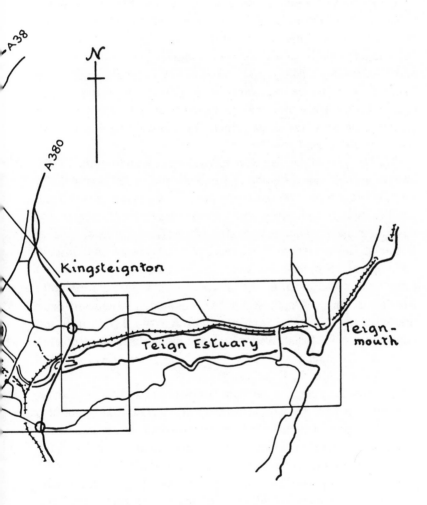

CHAPTER TWO

The Stover Canal

It was the development of the English pottery industry during the eighteenth century that created a need for china clay, and interest in beds of the deposited material existing in the Bovey valley. This particular form of kaolin is the result of erosion of the decomposed substance from the mass of Dartmoor granite and its carrying by natural forces to settle at the lower levels. Clay from this source became particularly valued for pottery working due to its plasticity and good casting quality, and because of the whiteness produced in firing. Extraction here has mainly been in the area extending south-east of Bovey Tracey towards Newton Abbot and the River Teign estuary, with workings located chiefly in the vicinities of Chudleigh Knighton and Kingsteignton.

The qualities of the clay were recognised at least from the 1730s, and from 1740 trade rose rapidly, from 385 tons in that year to 9,428 tons in 1784. Around two-thirds of production at this time was shipped via the Teign to the Mersey, some being thence carried on by inland navigation and packhorses to Staffordshire. Transport from the clay pits to the Newton Abbot quays was in those days slow and difficult. Although no more than four miles in direct distance there were no proper roads and much of the area was wet, boggy, and liable to flooding, so tortuous tracks had to be negotiated. Consequently there were limitations to shipments, which from 1765 included consignments for Josiah Wedgwood, and in the ability to respond to increased demands produced by the opening of the western section of the Trent & Mersey Canal in 1777.

The idea for a canal came from James Templer of Stover House, who envisaged good prospects from increasing clayworking, and also in the transport of lignite - a form of coal occurring in the Bovey basin -and of iron ore found in the granite hinterland and needing carriage to the coast for export to smelting works in Wales. Templer saw a canal as enabling also the import of coal, limestone, sea-sand for land improvement, and other goods, and thus as a benefit to farming. He was the eldest son of the earlier James Templer who, born of a poor Exeter family, after apprenticeship as a joiner had run away to sea, worked in Madras where he made a fortune and built docks, and then returned to England and his home county of Devon. Here he purchased from the Courtenay family the area of heathland on which he built a house and established the Stover estate. The younger James, who had been a Master in the Crown Office in London for thirty years, inherited the property on his father's death in 1782. Here he continued the work begun by his father in the development of the village of Teigngrace, including building of its church.

Cutting of the canal - the first in Devon since the sixteenth century Exeter Canal - began in January 1790, at Templer's own expense. His plan was to construct the waterway to Jewsbridge, near Heathfield, and from there up the Bovey valley to Bovey Tracey, with a branch eastwards to Chudleigh. However, as after two years' work under the engineer Thomas Grey of Exeter the canal reached only as far as Ventiford, at a cost of over £1,000, on 11 June 1792, Templer obtained a private Act (32 Geo III c.103) to enable him to raise £5,000 through mortgage of his estate, in order to complete the work. The powers were, however, never used, since the short canal was constructed only as far as Ventiford, a length of 1 $^7/_8$ miles.

In the course of its route the Stover Canal had to attain a rise totalling 19ft 3in, and this was achieved by five locks. The entrance to the canal at Newton Abbot was from the Whit Lake, or Whitelake, a tidal leat that drained this area of Jetty Marsh and which, deepened, provided a channel for boats coming up to Jetty Marsh Quay from the Teign estuary a quarter-mile or so downstream. The canal's entry point was from the northern bank of the Whitelake, through two stair-case locks which gave a combined rise of 6ft 6in. Both were originally constructed with earthen sides, but later Lock 1 was lined with brick-work and Lock 2 with timber. Granite was used for the sides of the gates. The gates, as on all the canal's locks, were 15ft wide, and depth above sill on these two was 5ft 9in. Lock 1 was enlarged to its eventual dimensions of 21ft length and 45ft width probably in 1841, so that it formed a basin for waiting craft. Lock 2 was 118ft long, and above it a weir was constructed to carry off excess water. Past the locks the canal was cut on a straight course north-westwards to the Fishwick area at Teignbridge, on the former main Newton-Exeter

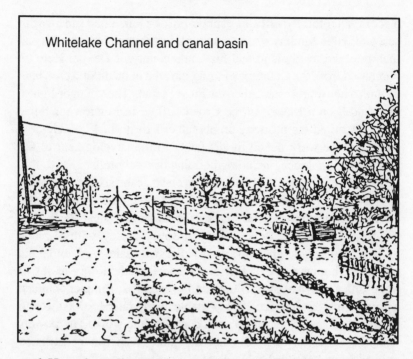

Whitelake Channel and canal basin

road. Here clay cellars were constructed alongside. The canal crossed the road (the present bridge was built in 1798) and by Lock 3 - 110ft long with 4ft 3in sill depth - was raised a further 6in. This lock was also originally earthen sided, later rebuilt with timber.

On the stretch to the next lock, about a third of a mile, the canal was watered from the east bank by the Fishwick Feeder - specially cut from the River Teign. Lock 4, called Graving Dock Lock, 56ft long with sill depth of 4ft 3in, was the shortest of the five, but effected the greatest rise, of 6ft 9in. Built (or rebuilt) of granite it was of more robust construction than the lower locks, with walling on the east side skilfully curved in later days to form a basin. Within a further eighth of a mile the canal reached Lock 5, at Teigngrace. This was also well built of granite (whether initially of this material or at the time of 1820s improvements is uncertain), 110ft in length with sill depth 5ft 6in and giving a rise of 5ft 6in. The half-mile summit level terminated at Ventiford. Here the canal widened to form a basin, with clay cellars built beside the wharf. Although the canal itself did not extend farther north as originally intended, a feeder channel was cut from the River Bovey at Jewsbridge to bring water to this point. Here it joined the Ventiford Brook, coming down from Stover, from which the supply for the canal was abstracted into the basin.

After two years' construction, of which the cost is not known, the Stover Canal was opened in 1792, and immediately began to prosper from the clay traffic. By 1795 seventeen barges were working on the Teign estuary, carrying cargoes down to the port of Teignmouth. Of these, ten, including the largest 35 ton vessels, used the Stover Canal. Seven of these barges were owned by James Templer himself.

By 1798 supplying of T.Wedgwood & Sons had been resumed, a trade which continued until 1815. In 1800 M.Dunsford wrote in *Miscellaneous observations in the Course of Tours through several parts of the West of England:*

> the conveyance of clay from thence to Liverpool, for the fine earthen manufacture of Staffordshire: it is dug in the parish of Kings-Teignton only, formed into little irregular squares somewhat like bricks, weighing thirty-six pounds each. About seven thousand tons are annually sent from these pits, in barges on Mr Templer's Canal, to the River Teign and down that river to the port, at 1s 6d per ton, toll and boatage, and there dispersed to the several manufacturers of Staffordshire;

(It was the rounding of the edges and corners of these cubes of clay during transit from the pits, due to its plasticity, that is reputed to have caused it to be termed 'ball clay').

The little canal was said to be of great benefit to the inland country by the returning of coal and other necessary commodities, and that the great part of the barren waste of Bovey Heathfield and lands near Stover were, in consequence, appearing like a 'new creation'. Land along the canal's route was reported to have tripled in value due to the aid to drainage that it provided and the consequent reduction of flooding.

Except for the few larger vessels, the standard barges using the canal were 50ft long and of 14ft beam, and carried 25 tons. They were not horse-drawn, but were either bow-hauled by the men, or sailed, using square, Viking-type rig. The trade on the Teign, which had stood at only 400 boatloads a year in 1790, rose steadily after the opening of the canal, increasing to 600 in 1816 and 1,000 in 1854. Perhaps somewhat resentful of the advantages their clay was giving to Staffordshire potters, and realising the facility for coal imports offered by the canal, in an attempt to compound their profits the Templers established an earthenware works on waste land at Indio, just south of Bovey Tracey, using clay from the same pits that were being worked for supplying Staffordshire, but the venture was not successful.

In 1813 James Templer died, and was succeeded in the estate by his son George. George Templer seems to have taken a more light-hearted view of life than his predecessors. He was a man of artistic talents, notably devoted to music and poetry, and was well-known in sporting pursuits, as master of the first regular pack of hounds in south Devon, and also as a pioneer of cricket. In business matters, however, he hardly excelled, although he must be credited with one notable achievement - construction of the Haytor Granite Tramway (see Chapter Three). The tramway, dating from 1820, brought increased traffic to the canal. Granite blocks, destined for London, carried from the high moor on the tramway were off-loaded on the wharf on the west side of the canal basin at Ventiford, or possibly hoisted by crane directly on to the barges, to start their waterborne journey. In 1821 the New Quay at Teignmouth was also built by George Templer to facilitate re-loading on to the bigger coastal vessels.

By 1829 George Templer's finances had fallen to a low level, and he sold the Stover estate including the canal (and the tramway) to Edward Seymour, 11th Duke of Somerset, a leading landowner in the area, who forthwith leased out the canal. The canal trade continued to flourish from carriage of both clay and granite and in 1836 the duke and others obtained an Act for improving the harbour at Teignmouth and also the Teign navigation up to the entrance of the Stover Canal. It seems likely that it was also around this time that the canal's first lock was enlarged to form a basin, and its walls improved, for a stone on the west wall of the lock bears the inscription: 'Duke of Somerset 1841'. This was a time of busy traffic on the Teign estuary. One of the other developments was the construction by Lord Clifford, owner of Ugbrooke House and of most of the clay workings on the north-east side of the River Teign, of the short Hackney Canal (see Chapter Four).

In the late 1850s the trade in Haytor granite ceased, and at the

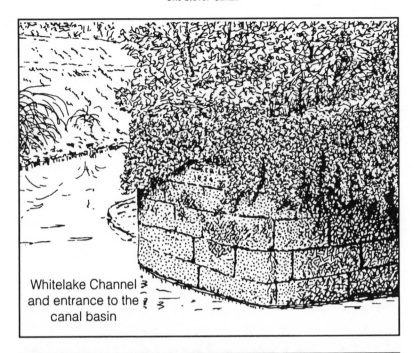

Whitelake Channel
and entrance to the
canal basin

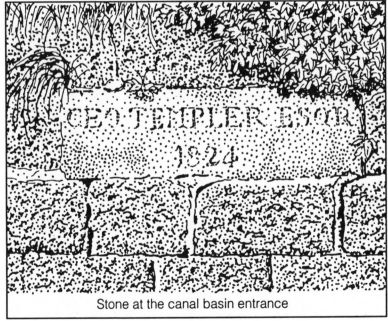

Stone at the canal basin entrance

same time plans were proceeding towards the construction of a railway to Moretonhampstead through this area of the Duke of Somerset's land. As a result of negotiations, in 1862 the canal was sold by the duke to the railway company, with no requirement for its maintenance above Teignbridge. Following the opening of the railway in 1866 the canal was held by lessees up to 1942 (see Chapter Five).

From 1870 only the length of canal up to Graving Dock Lock was used - a distance of 1 $^{1}/_{4}$ miles. Traffic here continued, however, well into the twentieth century, with the clay trade increasing up to the early 1900s. Gradually, though, road transport took over the carriage of clay, and in 1939 use of the Stover Canal came to an end.

CHAPTER THREE

The quarries, and the Haytor Granite Tramway

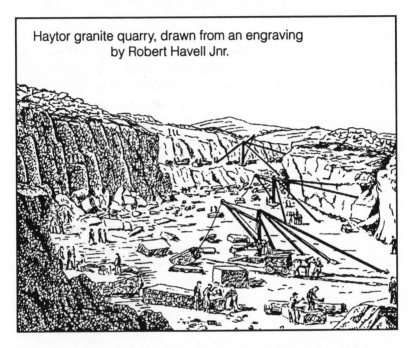

Haytor granite quarry, drawn from an engraving
by Robert Havell Jnr.

It would be interesting if we could know the precise circumstances which led to granite from Dartmoor being sought for buildings in London in the early part of the nineteenth century. Truly this was a time of considerable construction in the capital, as elsewhere, but why look to Dartmoor when, for example, the shipping of Portland stone from the Dorset coast had long been established, and since Bath stone had become more easily available due to inland navigation developments? Remoteness of the granite sources, and this rock's hardness in working can hardly have made its use an easy prospect.

How Dartmoor granite - and that from Haytor in particular - came to be used for prominent London structures we shall probably never know. But perhaps appraisal of other developments on Dartmoor at that time may give some clues. Here, as in other parts of Britain, the period from the late eighteenth century and through the first half of the nineteenth century was one of awakening, growth and inventiveness. The exploitation of Dartmoor was proceeding, with the arrival of so-called 'improvers' with optimistic ideas and plans for taming the wilderness by farming, and marketing the resources. Granite working which had long been done for local needs was increasing, particularly on the western side of the moor for the building of Princetown. Quarrying techniques developed around 1800 eased the taking. London connections of the improvers, including Thomas Tyrwhitt - pioneer of Princetown and friend of the Prince of Wales, holder of the Duchy of Cornwall lands on the moor - must have caused Dartmoor granite to be spoken of in high places, and its strength, weight-bearing ability and good weathering qualities extolled. George Templer could hardly have been unaware of possibilities presented by his own rock sources, if only they could be brought within reach of his already existing canal.

Up to this stage horses and carts had been the form of transport used for carrying granite down the rough twisty tracks from Haytor. Clearly this was slow and far too limited if shipping of the stone was to become a commercial proposition. Undoubtedly it was Templer's awareness of the considerable demand for stone created by building developments in London and elsewhere that concentrated his thought on the transport problem, and then, apparently, a contract he obtained for supplying stone for the construction of London Bridge, designed by John Rennie to replace the medieval structure, which precipitated his decision to build a tramway.

Tramways had been devised and used over the two previous centuries, initially for transporting coal in areas of the Midlands and Tyneside. In the sixteenth and seventeenth centuries the rails were of wood, later faced with iron plates for durability, but by 1767 iron rails cast at Coalbrookdale were being used for transport in that area and in south Wales. At first these were all of the 'edge rail' type, designed to carry trucks with flanged wheels. From about 1780, however, the flange was transferred to rails - 'L' shaped in section - for taking plain wheeled waggons, and this style found notable favour in Wales. In this latter part of the eighteenth century many tramways were constructed to serve canals, generally for carrying the products of mineral extraction. An example is the Peak Forest Tramway, built

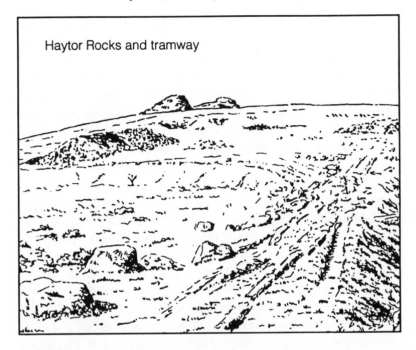

Haytor Rocks and tramway

in the 1790s, which connected limestone quarries near Buxton in Derbyshire with the Peak Forest and Ashton-under-Lyne Canals. Its rails were L-section, laid on stone slabs with stone sleepers.

Iron rails were certainly not unknown in the south-west, despite the distance from main iron-working areas. Their use had been suggested in the 1790s by the engineers John and George Nuttall, in conjunction with the proposed Bude Canal on which they were reporting. Work did not proceed then, but when building of the canal began in 1819 iron rails were provided for the wheeled boats on the six inclined planes, as they had been a few years earlier for carriage on the incline of the Tavistock Canal at Morwellham. And, on the western side of Dartmoor, the Plymouth & Dartmoor Railway, also being constructed in the early 1820s, mainly for granite transport, used cast iron rails laid in cast-iron chairs bolted to granite blocks which acted as sleepers. (Granite blocks were indeed also used here, however, for sidings, but they differed from those on the Haytor tramway, having their inner edges specially cut for taking the flanged wheels of the waggons).

Templer, therefore, had plenty of precedents to consider in his plans for a tramway. Whether or not it was his own original idea to use granite for the actual rails, or that of an adviser, again we do not know. In the outcome it was evidently the abundance of suitable granite that won the day, together with an undoubted degree of pioneering spirit, ingenuity, and available labour and skill. Certainly the structure of the Haytor Granite Tramway, with granite blocks forming the rails, cut with a rebate for carrying the plain iron wheels of the waggons, was most unusual. And (with the exception of one other slightly similar example - the $^1/_8$ mile 3ft gauge limestone railway at Conisborough, Doncaster) it presents a system that was quite unique.

The area of Ilsington parish which includes Haytor Rocks and the surrounding down - in medieval times part of the Manor of Ilsington -on which five quarries were developed, had been purchased in the eighteenth century by George Templer's grandfather. Actual quarrying was not properly initiated before the early years of the nineteenth century, so it is probable that the considerable quantities of granite carted down from here for the building of Stover House, and other constructions, was mainly from detached surface rock or 'clitter'. Of this there must have been an abundance, as is characteristic around most Dartmoor tors, with plenty covering the now mainly cleared area around Hay Tor - or 'Haytor Rocks' - as well as elsewhere.

It is likely, therefore, that early stone for Stover was taken from around the actual Hay Tor, and possibly also from the rocky area near the western edge of the Down, north of Saddle Tor, above Emsworthy, which is still rich in clitter. Both sides would have enabled relatively easy downhill access on tracks southward to the Widecombe-Bovey road across the moor. Two small quarries were eventually developed on these western rocks, one at the extreme west end, which had two faces, and the other to the east known as Harrow Barrow with three. Both were connected by branches with the tramway's main trunk to the north-east. The order and dates of development of the five separate quarries is not known. Opening-up a new quarry takes some little while, with preliminary excavation, removal of overburden, and establishment of the working area and necessary buildings and equipment. One may wonder if perhaps these small western areas of extraction may have pre-dated the major quarry, and

Holwell Tor Quarry. From an original print by T.H.Williams, dated 1829.
Reproduced by kind permission of the owner,
Mr J.V.Somers Cocks.

possibly even have provided initial tramway blocks. Opinions differ, but it is hard to believe that, once the main quarry was opened and in production, back tracking involving about a mile of tramway to much more modest workings of lesser potential would have been embarked upon.

The other two quarries of the group consisted of Holwell, and 'Rubble Heap'. Holwell Quarry, situated at a lower level to the north-west, on the north side of Holwell Tor, was served by its own half-mile branch of tramway, and with its high rockface was obviously the source of much good quality production. Rubble Heap Quarry, north-west of Haytor Rocks, which displays a sizeable circular face, is approached along a narrow cutting through which the tramway branch passed to serve the workings. The large tips alongside display much evidence of granite cutting and shaping.

The Act of Parliament for the rebuilding of London Bridge specified types of British granite that were to be used in its construction. For the exterior of the bridge itself, the east side was to be of purple

Aberdeen, the western side of light grey 'Devonshire Haytor', with the uniting arch stone of red brown Peterhead. No doubt assurance of a demand for supplies for this particular contract, and also for others, encouraged George Templer to develop his resources. There was no Act for the Haytor Granite Tramway. Templer constructed it on his own land at his own expense, and the identity of the engineer is not known. Neither is there any precise record of the cost, but it is believed to have been over £30,000. Considering the amount of work needed in order to survey and prepare the route, and in cutting and shaping the setts and laying them in place, the operation must have been started well in advance of the tramway's opening date of 16 September 1820. This important occasion was marked by great festivities on Haytor Down, with bands, speeches, collation, and dancing, all at George Templer's expense. The *Exeter Flying Post* of 21 September 1820 described the proceedings thus:

> On Saturday Mr Templer, of Stover House, gave a grand fete champetre on Haytor Down, on the completion of the granite rail-road. The company assembled at its foot on Bovey Heathfield, and in procession passed over it to the rock. A long string of carriages, filled with elegant and beautiful females, multitudes of horsemen, workmen on foot, the wagons covered with laurels and waving streamers, formed in their windings through the valley an attractive scene to spectators on the adjacent hill. Old Haytor seemed alive; its sides were lined with groups of persons, and on its top a proud flag fluttered in the wind. Previously to returning to dine, Mr Templer addressed the assemblage in a short and energetic speech, which excited bursts of applause. He stated the causes that induced him to engage in such a great undertaking. He pointed out the advantages which it offered to the surrounding proprietors, the employment it would find for the mechanic and labourer, and its tendency to increase to a great degree the trade of the port of Teignmouth. In averting to the Plymouth railway, he expressed his hope that both might prosper, and not endanger, by improper rivalry, the success of either.

(The 'improper rivalry' undoubtedly relates to the Plymouth & Dartmoor Railway currently being built. Its main length was opened in 1823 but the entirety not until a little later).

The main trunk of the Haytor Granite Tramway from the quarries on Haytor Down to the Stover Canal at Ventiford covered a distance of 8 $\frac{1}{2}$ miles, but it is estimated that if the lengths of the various branches and sidings were added the total would be around 10 miles. Over this 8$\frac{1}{2}$ miles the tramway had to negotiate a descent of 1,300ft.

From the main quarry, $\frac{1}{4}$ mile north of Haytor Rocks, the tramway took off northwards to join the route running west-east across the Down. Besides the now most noticeable line from the quarry there were others that deviated, and one that ran north-westward from the quarry to join the trunk near and opposite the junction of the line ascending from Holwell Quarry. Also to the west the tramway connected with branches from Rubble Heap Quarry and the two smaller ones near Emsworthy. The tramway proceeded eastwards to the edge of the Down, but then curved north-westwards along the contour, close to another small (non-granite) quarry, and then curved again towards the east through the Yarner area. Continuing its gradual descent the tramway became established on a fairly direct south-eastward course as it ran south of Bovey Tracey and then almost parallel with and south of the River Bovey across Bovey Heath. Its route passed east of the Templers' residence at Stover on the approach to Ventiford, where it ended at the basin of the Stover Canal.

The granite blocks which formed the tramway were not standard in size. They were of about 5ft average length, but varied from 4ft to

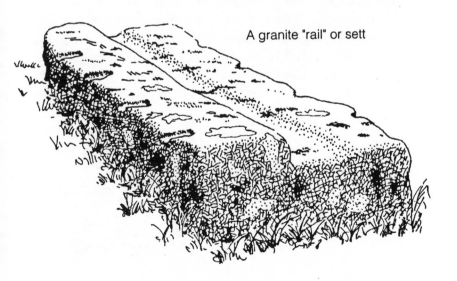

A granite "rail" or sett

8ft, and on curves quite short lengths of setts were used. Squarish in section, the blocks had an average width of 12-15in and depth of about 10in. They were cut on the upper surface, about 7in from the inner edge, to provide a 3in deep rebate, forming a longitudinal flange on which ran the plain iron wheels of the waggons, having a gauge of 4ft 3in. At junctions of branches and sidings the blocks were so cut with grooves to form 'points', enabling the alternative lines to be taken. There is plenty of evidence on the route to show how skilfully this was done. The horses were guided in the right direction, but a special device was used to assist the waggons on to the desired route. The drilled hole into which this was inserted is visible in several examples of the pointwork. Many of the setts were marked with numbers, or initials - presumably of the men who cut them.

The small low waggons were flat topped, and believed to have been about 13ft long by 10ft wide, with their flangeless wheels measuring 2ft in diameter and having 3in width on tread. They were formed into trains of about twelve waggons, the leading one being equipped with shafts. Horses drew the trains, or restrained them from the rear as necessary on the descent. While the ascending line from Holwell Quarry needed the strength of several horses - it was said that nineteen stout shires drew the stone, mounted on 12-wheeled carts, up from here - the main length of the route was downhill, so braking was a necessity. However, although the overall fall was quite considerable it was mainly fairly gradual, and the construction seems to have been so devised to provide impetus on the descending route but also a degree of friction between the rough granite and small wheels that would help to impede runaway. It seems that a strong 10ft-12ft pole may also have been used as a brake, applied to the rim of a wheel.

Many men worked in the actual quarrying, as well as on the tramway and in other ancillary activities. One may imagine, for example, the scene within the large area of the main Haytor Quarry, on the floor of which sections of the tramway ran to the various faces. At the rockface large blocks of granite were extracted by the use of gunpowder and by men wielding picks. The noise must have been considerable. Blocks would then be hoisted by cranes and moved to points where they could be split and cut into required shapes. The splitting of the granite was done by the method known as 'feather and tare', which had replaced the former wedge-and-groove process around the year 1800. In the feather and tare method a series of holes was made along the line of potential fracture of the rock by means of a tool called a 'jumper'. Into these holes pairs of 'feathers' - partial-hoop shaped pieces of metal - were inserted, and between each pair of feathers a piece of wedge-shaped metal - the 'tare' - was placed.

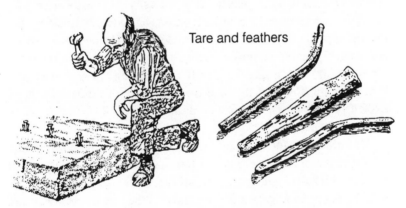

Tare and feathers

The tares were hammered in succession until the block of granite broke apart. Much evidence of such cutting exists, both in the quarries and on the surrounding turf, in the form of half-round holes along the cleavage line of split granite. (The same method is still employed in granite working). Signs of cutting and dressing are also seen in the large quantities of granite chips lying around. These are particularly abundant in the vicinity of Rubble Heap Quarry, where, it is believed, additional waste was dumped from the main Haytor Quarry.

Some remains of buildings also exist in the form of ruined walls and platform bases. These would have included working buildings, and also dwellings. A number of these were sited around the area of the main quarry, but the most interesting set of remains lies just north of the western Harrow Barrow Quarry. They comprise a rectangular enclosure, covering just over $1/8$ acre, within which are the remains of several buildings. These were apparently workers' dwellings during the early years of the industry here. Later George Templer provided more comfortable accommodation in cottages at Haytor Vale.

In 1825 George Templer formed a company of the Proprietors of the Devon Haytor Quarries. Later this became a joint stock company with offices in Broad Street, London, and capital of £200,000. By now the company was sending away several thousand tons of granite annually for use in the construction of buildings in London that included the British Museum and the National Gallery, and also - at around this time or soon after - for London's New Goldsmiths' Hall, New Fishmongers' Hall and Covent Garden Market, for Ramsgate Harbour monument, for pedestals for Pitt's statue in Hanover Square, London, and George IV's in Edinburgh, and also in Buckingham Palace, as well as for much other notable work. The demands caused considerably increased traffic on the Stover Canal, with carriage rising to 20,000 tons a year. Evidently anticipating yet greater expansion the company paid the land-owning Duke of Somerset rent of £200 a year for the right to extend its area and work 600 acres, but in fact only 90 acres were worked.

Unfortunately for Templer, however, prosperity did not last, and the expenses of his generous and hospitable life-style overtook his fortunes. He had to reduce his pleasure activities, and in January 1829 sold the house and estate at Stover, and also the Haytor Tramway and the Stover Canal to the 11th Duke of Somerset. For a short while George Templer retired from the scene, but he returned and built himself a mansion, called Sandford Orleigh, at Newton Abbot, in which he took up residence. He also re-entered the granite business, becoming the Haytor company's chief agent in Devon. The company, however, was soon suffering severe financial problems, attributed to inefficiencies amongst its staff, very strong competition from keener businesses, and an accounting system verging on bankruptcy. The troubles were a source of much worry to John Bigg, the company's agent and secretary in London, as has been shown by letters between him and Templer written in 1833-4. Bigg, it seems, had repeatedly to report to the directors his lack of funds for settling accounts, and Templer appears to have been given the blame, being regarded as lacking in business skills and having too easy a discipline in the matter of expenses and the collection of dues, as well as failing to answer correspondence. Reports that cartloads of building stone worth 30 shillings were being sold for 6 pence reinforced Bigg's regard of Templer's incompetence.

The company was losing contracts, and in the year of the correspondence only a single major one was secured - for the Atlas Fire Office. Furthermore this suffered from late deliveries and through expensive adjustments having to be made, because stones had been cut to incorrect measurements. Apart from other grievances the company's right to work the quarries was becoming uncertain. Bigg questioned Templer as to whether he had conveyed by deed his property to the Duke of Somerset, if he had reserved or had a lease granted to him for the 25 years of the Haytor Quarries which he had leased to the Haytor Granite Company. Bigg stated that he himself was persuaded that Templer took care in selling the Fee of Haytor Down to have the reservation to protect the company, but other people were thinking differently, asserting that he had sold to the duke absolutely what he had previously leased to the company. To this Templer failed to reply until pressed by the directors in the face of legal action by the duke. Amid accusations of defaulting in the payment to workers only the complicated situation regarding the leases served to keep the company intact.

In March 1834 the possibility of a contract for carrying iron ore on the tramway was being considered. The ore would come from the Haytor Iron Mine in Haytor Vale which was currently productive. Bigg asked Templer for his views on contracting for carrying the ore down the railroad to Ventiford, either on behalf of the Haytor company or himself. If the transport was to be undertaken new waggons would be needed with high sides rather than the flat vehicles used for carrying stone. Although George Templer probably had connections with the Haytor Iron Company there is no indication that any contract for transporting the ore on the tramway ensued.

There was apparently no production of granite from the Haytor

Quarries throughout the 1840s, during which, in December 1843, George Templer died as the result of a hunting accident. This stoppage was due to letting of the quarries by the Duke of Somerset in the late 1830s to Johnson Brothers, rivals of the Haytor company, who were currently working the quarries at Swell Tor, King Tor and Foggintor on Walkhampton Common, on the western side of Dartmoor. The granite there being of inferior quality to that of Haytor, Johnsons had earlier failed in efforts to gain a contract for supplying stone for London Bridge. When Johnsons gained their 7-year lease from the Duke of Somerset they proceeded to close down the quarries at Haytor and to rename their own enterprise as the Haytor Granite Company, evidently as a form of deception to enhance marketing appeal of their established production. The duke refused to renew the lease when the seven years expired.

After a decade in which many unemployed quarry workers and their families had left Haytor Vale, by 1850 the Haytor quarries were again being worked under the Duke of Somerset and said to be employing 100 people, due to a sustained demand for granite for bridges, quays and other construction. But through the 1850s demand and production dwindled, and by 1858 had virtually ceased, with the tramway disused. The main factor in the decline must undoubtedly have been the competition from granite quarries elsewhere, particularly those on the western side of the moor and in Cornwall, where easier access to the sea made export less costly. The double handling of the Haytor granite necessitated by the transfer from tramway to canal at Ventiford added to the expense. It was also of significance that 1858 was the year in which the Newton & Moretonhampstead Railway was promoted.

Working of the quarries ceased after 1865, apart from the occasional cutting of stone for special requirements. However, they were re-opened again at the very end of the century, leased by the Duke of Somerset to the Exeter firm of J.Easton & Son. The tramway, though, remained unused, the stone being transported by tractor to Bovey Tracey. A tender submitted at this time for supplying granite for the widening of London Bridge was lost by Haytor when the contract was awarded to Pethick & Company of Plymouth, who were currently working at Swell Tor.

In 1919 Haytor granite was used for Exeter's War Memorial, and it was said that carrying the cut stone down from the quarries took twice the time that would have been taken by the tramway.

An ambitious plan was put forward in 1905 for the construction of an electric tramway along the old granite route as a tourist attraction for visitors to the tor. Power was to be supplied in the form of electricity generated by a dynamo driven by producer gas, to be manufactured by burning Bovey lignite. A generating station had even been built, but this was adapted for industry when the scheme failed to materialise.

The eventual outcome for Haytor Down and the granite tramway is undoubtedly more acceptable to most people's enjoyment. In 1975 the Down was purchased from the Leighon Estate by the Dartmoor National Park Authority, and the main length of the tramway upon it is now scheduled as an Ancient Monument.

In addition to the freedom on the Down much of the route below is also accessible by public footpaths.

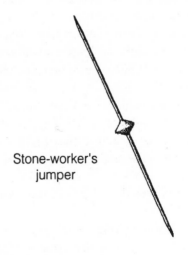

Stone-worker's
jumper

CHAPTER FOUR

The waterway of the Teign

Barge on the Teign

Up to the end of the eighteenth century salt marshes covered the area between Newton Abbot and Kingsteignton at the head of the Teign estuary, and in the estuary itself silting was a persistant problem to navigation. This became a matter of particular concern as the clay and granite export business developed. In the 1830s the necessity for remedial measures was discussed between the owners of the river bed: the Duke of Somerset who owned clay pits and the Stover Canal, Lord Clifford who had pits to the north, and the Earl of Devon, Lord of the Manor of East Teignmouth. They commissioned a report from the engineer and surveyor J.B.West, who estimated the cost of removing the bar at the Teignmouth harbour entrance, and improving and deepening the navigation of the River Teign so that the channel would be as deep as the sill of the lock of the Stover Canal at Jetty Marsh, at £3,967 17s 5d, and for the work to take five years. This was accepted, and an Act sought and obtained on 19 May 1836 (6 William IV cap xlii).

Although Teignmouth was a subsidiary within the port area of Exeter, commissioners were appointed for the harbour, including *ex officio* the Lords of the Manors of East and West Teignmouth, and the owner of the Stover Canal. Others comprised local property owners, including George Templer, holder of the largest manor at Newton. The commissioners' powers gave them jurisdiction to the point of high water at ordinary spring tides.

Under the terms of the Act the commissioners were required to cut, deepen, scour, cleanse, extend, widen and make more navigable the river and navigation from the Stover Canal to the sea, to the depth specified by West. They were to widen and deepen the navigable channel sufficiently for vessels plying between canal and harbour to pass each other safely and easily. And they were to construct piers, walls or embankments as necessary for securing and preserving the works and navigation from the sea.

In addition the commissioners were to be responsible for providing buoys to indicate the channels and to erect lighthouses. There were, however, delays in fulfilling these obligations - the small lighthouse on the Den, its red light a warning to vessels approaching around the Nose and a guide to those entering the Teign, was not built until 1844-5, and buoys - nine above Coombe Cellars and eleven below - were not placed until 1922.

The Act authorised the raising of £12,000, if necessary by mortgage of expected tolls, and the taking of tolls on the river. Subscribers numbered just eleven, consisting of:-

Name	Place of abode	Quality or calling	Amount
Somerset	Stover house	Duke	£1,000
Devon	Powderham Castle	Earl	£100
John Chappel Tozer	Teignmouth	Gentleman	£100
W.Vallance	Newton	Merchant	£100
J.Vicary	Newton	Woolstapler	£100
W.Langmead	Elford Leigh	Esquire	£100
W.Watts	Kingsteignton	Clerk	£100
Sam.Whiteway	Kingsteignton	Merchant	£100
W.H.Tomkin	Chudleigh	Esquire	£100
Thomas Pinseul	Kingsteignton	Gentleman	£100
W.Blount	London	Esquire	£100

Since these subscriptions totalled only £2,000, advantage was apparently taken of permission to borrow funds from the Commissioner of Works.

For improvement of the harbour it was proposed to remove the Bench Rocks, and advice was sought from Sir John Rennie, who recommended dredging the entrance channel. Screw moorings were laid near Randalls Quay and in Shaldon Pool. Nevertheless, the dangerous bar - which had necessitated compulsory pilotage from 1825 - remained a constant challenge, despite continued works. Dredging was tried in 1857, further operations including building a 330yd sand-arresting groyne were carried out in 1865, in 1869 more rocks were removed, and in 1906 a mechanical sand-blower was used.

West's plan was followed precisely in the improvements of the actual estuary, which consisted mainly of dredging existing or new channels where necessary. On the deeply curved entrance from the harbour mouth dredging was not needed, but upstream, where the channel divided, the northern course was initially deepened until direction difficulties ensued. By cutting through sandbanks the dredging operations were therefore brought towards the south bank near Coombe Cellars, and continued mainly on this line until reaching the junction of the north and south channels of the Teign near the one to Hackney Quay. More dredging was needed here and on the Teign's main southerly line, past Newton Abbot's early quay on the south bank and right up to the Whitelake Channel. The banks of the river estuary were considered high enough to obviate any need for piles.

Navigation in the estuary was greatly dependent on the state of the tide, since the river's outflow divided into various streams which were often reduced to trickles. Therefore vessels had to make the most of the time approaching high tide and the early hours of the ebb. That spell was often busy with craft working to and from the various quays, carrying all kinds of goods and produce. The Teign barges were striking in appearance, and with their square Viking-style sails virtually unique in the area. The wooden barges were 5ft deep and had flat bottoms, round bows and flat transom sterns. Generally the sails provided sufficient impetus for the laden barges travelling downstream, but poles would be used if winds were slack on the return. It was a hard life for the men who worked them, and demanded toughness of character.

At the upper area of the estuary, besides the quays at Jetty Marsh and the basin of the Stover Canal, there were others. As well as Newton Abbot's ancient Town Quay at the point where the River Lemon joins the Teign, from 1835, until obliteration by the Moretonhampstead railway in the 1860s, the town had another wharf sited on an artificial cut made from the Teign towards the Kingsteignton road. There were also proposals to construct a half-mile canal from below Town Quay on the Teign into the centre of Newton Abbot. A plan for this was submitted in 1827 by James Green, engineer of the recently completed Bude Canal and shortly after of the Grand Western Canal and others. The Newton canal was intended to have a tide-lock at its entrance and a basin at the point where Queen Street, Station Road, and The Avenue meet, but the plan was not proceeded with.

Another canal did however come into being to connect with the Teign - the Hackney or Kingsteignton Canal. This was constructed by Lord Clifford of Chudleigh to facilitate the export of clay by workers of the pits on his land in the area of Chudleigh Knighton, Preston and Kingsteignton, and so to enable them to compete more equally with clay producers in the Bovey basin who had long had the benefit of the Stover Canal. Previously the clay from Lord Clifford's land had been exported down the Teign from Hackney Quay, to which it was conveyed by packhorses. Loading the clay on to the boats here often presented difficulties due to the considerable variations of tide. Consequently the decision was taken to build a canal of $^5/_8$ mile from the channel of the Teign near Hackney Quay to a point beside the present Newton Abbot-Kingsteignton road. A tidal lock was constructed at the entrance from the Teign, 108ft 3in long and 14ft wide, with 3ft 5in on sill, and at the terminus a basin with adjacent clay cellars. The distance by horse transport of the clay was thus reduced by nearly a mile, and the loading of the boats made much easier. It appears that the boats were owned by Lord Clifford himself, and his clay tenants were required to transport all their production by this means. After two years' building the Hackney Canal opened on 7 March 1843, and continued in use until 1928.

In order to finance the undertaking the Harbour Commissioners were more concerned with the collection of tolls from ships of 80-300 tons using the harbour, which off-loaded on to lighters whilst at anchor, than with the less remunerative river trade. But there was incompetence amongst members and their system was not very efficient. Also, Teignmouth suffered from a certain disadvantage in being a subsidiary of the port of Exeter, which collected dues, and this was a matter which caused six official complaints between 1832 and 1853. Eventually, when the matter was considered in Parliament, the Commissioners were £5,600 in debt. As a remedial measure the original Act was repealed, and after three years' grace a new body of Commissioners was established, comprising eighteen of the original members, two from the Admiralty, the Lord of the Manor of East Teignmouth and the Lord of the Manor of West Teignmouth, and the respective owners of the Stover and Hackney Canals, plus four representatives of the shipowners and eight of the harbour ratepayers.

Under the new system jurisdiction was extended beyond the original harbour, which was bounded by two stones, each marked T.H.B.- one by the Ness and the other on the shore of the Den, so that the Port of Teignmouth was extended from Galmpton Point (thus including Torquay and Paignton but not Brixham) to Langstone Point beyond Dawlish. The Commissioners were also granted enhanced financial powers, and Exeter was compensated for loss of revenue. The arrangements met with favour in Teignmouth, which marked the outcome with celebrations.

From then on Teignmouth appears to have flourished, not just as a port but also in the development of shipbuilding. And from the mid-nineteenth century the considerable attractions of this seaside town and its hinterland became increasingly recognised as it grew into a resort that continues to bring trade to the town.

CHAPTER FIVE

Railway advance and the changing scene

During the 1850s, with the demand for Haytor granite declining due to competition from more easily exportable sources, and with prospects of railway advance up the Teign and Bovey valleys, the interest of the Duke of Somerset in his canal, and in the granite tramway, waned.

In 1858 the Newton & Moretonhampstead Railway Company was incorporated and a survey made for the line, from a junction with the South Devon Railway at Newton Abbot (established here since 1846) to Bovey Tracey, Lustleigh and Moretonhampstead. In 1861 the company was reconstituted under its chairman, the Earl of Devon, as the Moretonhampstead & South Devon Railway Company. It was planned to take the railway's route through the centre of the Stover estate, which necessitated negotiations with the duke. Here the Duke of Somerset saw a potential advantage in persuading the railway company to purchase the Stover Canal - not that its sale, unless at a good price, would bring any long-term advantage, since he would actually lose income from its leaseholders, but because he felt he might also be able to include the lower length of the Haytor Granite Tramway as part of the deal. After some persuasion, and recognition of the efficiency of the canal in transporting clay, agreement was reached, and in 1862 the railway company purchased the canal and the section of the tramway on its planned line from the duke, for £8,000. Under the agreement the railway company had no obligations to maintain the canal above Teignbridge or the section of the granite tramway - a distance of just over a mile - on its route. The company was required, however, to construct and maintain a siding and crane near the point where the tramway diverged from the new railway, presumably for continued granite use. The facility was provided, and known as the Bovey Granite Siding, but it is doubtful if it was ever used in the way intended.

During the immediately ensuing construction of the railway, the railway company was approached by others in the neighbourhood on the possibility of canal purchase. The interested parties were Watts,

Blake & Co, a father and son partnership who, besides working clay pits on their family land at Preston Manor, had bought other areas of clay-workings for their expanding business, and Mr Whiteway, acting on behalf of Mr Knight, lessee of the Hackney Canal. They were informed, however, that the railway company had no current plans for disposing of the canal.

Trade on the lower section of the canal continued much as before, but with the lessees Whiteway & Mortimer (of whom Mr Whiteway was also manager) now paying their rents to the railway company instead of to the duke. Meanwhile, above Lock 3 at Teignbridge the canal became unused, since the wharf for clay - the only commodity now being carried -was immediately below it, south of the bridge. However, in the building of the railway the pile of the canal's dry dock at Teigngrace had been destroyed, leaving the lessees without repair facilities. Since the next upper level of the canal was still effectively watered by the Fishwick Feeder the owners therefore agreed to construct a new dock on the east side of Lock 4. This work proceeded, and the lock became known as Graving Dock Lock.

Construction of the 12 $\frac{1}{4}$ mile broad gauge railway was completed, and opened on 4 July 1866. It had a rise from 50ft to 588ft, with maximum gradient of 1 in 50. Although, in accordance with specifications, all the bridges on its route were made wide enough to carry double rails, the line was of single track throughout. Before its completion, however, the railway company faced financial problems, since the eventual cost rose to £155,000 - half as much again as the originally authorised capital - and there were difficulties in raising the additional sum.

Soon after the opening of the railway the date for renewal of the canal lease was approaching. Mr Watts notified that his firm would be willing to take a lease for seven or fourteen years, but the railway company decided to offer to continue that of the present lessees for a further year. This was to be under existing terms, except that it was suggested that Jetty Marsh Quay could revert to the Duke of Somerset. However, this was refused. There was also concern regarding failure by the lessees to comply with a notice from the owners requiring canal works to be carried out. Consequently, after deliberations the railway company advertised in the press for tenders for a three-year lease from 1 May 1867. In the outcome the company rejected the tender received from the current leaseholders Whiteway & Mortimer (£325) and that of J.Bearne, who later amalgamated with Watts & Blake (£405), and accepted the offer of Watts Blake & Co who tendered £460. The former lessees were ordered to repair the Ventiford cellars before relinquishing.

As Watts and company proceeded in their first three year period of working the canal they approached the railway company regarding the lease's extension. After some delay the figure of £5,250 for a ten-year lease was suggested by the railway, but declined by the clay firm. Considering that their original tender had been too high, Watts and company now offered £330 a year, but this was rejected by the owners, and so the firm declined to continue its lease after expiry. Eventually however the railway company was unable to find anyone else to take on the canal, so a new lease was issued to Watts at the rate of £330 per annum as latterly tendered.

In 1872 the railway was absorbed by the South Devon Railway Company, and this in turn was purchased by the Great Western Railway following authorisation in 1877. (The GWR noted in 1896 that it had paid £2,800 for the Stover Canal). The station previously known as Chudleigh Road was renamed Heathfield when in 1882 the Teign Valley Railway was added to the system, with a station nearer the town of Chudleigh. In 1904 the link was completed through to Exeter, which increased the railway's traffic. Exactly how the railway developments affected the leasing of the canal in the immediately following years is uncertain, but a new lease was granted by the GWR to Watts and company for 21 years from Michaelmas 1893. Under its terms the clay firm was to maintain the canal and also ten boats owned by the GWR, which was to have the power to use the canal for trade but not so as to interfere with the lessees. It appeared from the lease that continued granite traffic was expected on the canal, also that of ironstone and iron ore by the executors of George Templer, but this would have been an impracticable impossibility by this stage when the canal's upper reach had become disused and overgrown.

Besides using the GWR barges Watts, Blake, Bearne & Co apparently also built their own 25 ton boats, and on the return trip from Teignmouth they carried coal and builders' materials which were unloaded on Jetty Marsh Quay. A GWR report of 1896 indicated that the Stover Canal's lower section was well watered and well maintained. It was said to be the only canal owned by the GWR where income exceeded expenditure. Repairs on the canal, which occasionally necessitated stoppages of the traffic, and ordinary maintenance carried out as convenient by lightermen, incurred an average cost to the clay company of £386 a year. In the early 1900s they had to spend £500 on new lock gates and other works. By this time it was becoming realised by WBB & Co that they were operating at a loss, in the GWR's favour, and that the canal had become unremunerative, although it was still the best means of carrying clay. Locally there were complaints that the lessees exercised a monopoly over firms having to take barges down the estuary to Teignmouth. However, it was stated by WBB that they were always willing to carry goods for the public and that anyway there was very little traffic other than their own.

Improvements to the port of Teignmouth were carried out in the latter part of the nineteenth century and in the twentieth, when the trade in clay increased. WBB's lease from the GWR was renewed for fourteen-year terms, in 1914 and 1928. The latter period would have run until 1942, but before that the canal was disused.

In the 1930s it was still possible to see the barges being towed down the Teign by the tug *Kestrel*, but road transport of dehydrated and powdered clay was taking over. The Hackney Canal became unused from 1928, while the Stover Canal, having the advantage of connecting directly from clay pit to port, continued until 1939.

In 1943 the GWR proceeded to close the Stover Canal to navigation and so to be free of the obligation to maintain it. As for the railways, the Teign Valley line was closed in 1958, the route from Heathfield to Moretonhampstead in 1959. Between Newton Abbot and Heathfield the line remains open, used now solely by an oil company for transport to its Heathfield depot.

CHAPTER SIX

Following the route

Unfinished cider pound base

THE HAYTOR GRANITE TRAMWAY

A convenient location from which to commence exploration of the Haytor Granite Tramway on Haytor Down is the car park west of Haytor Vale, at SX 765771. From here the main quarry is situated $1/3$ - $1/2$ mile across the Down to the north-west (north of the tor), at SX 760775. At the edge of the quarry area near three trees, close to a walled enclosure and gatepost on the south-west side, where there are vestiges of former habitations, is a wire fence with an entrance gate. The site within, bounded by a series of imposing rockfaces, is strewn with boulders and contains a pond, with rough pathways giving access around it. The fallen boom of a derrick and an abandoned winch are reminders of the heavy work involved in hoisting the cut blocks on to the tramway waggons. The scene, which would have been busy and noisy in the quarry's working days, is now generally tranquil, and the pond and its surroundings are a haven for wildlife.

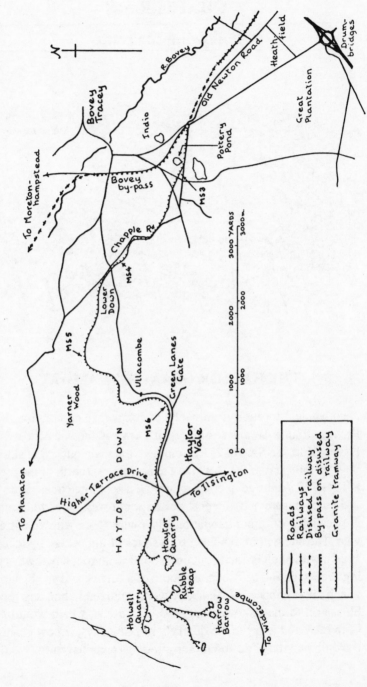

Haytor Granite Tramway

Leaving the quarry near the point of entry, remains of the tramway become apparent. Beyond an elongated tip of quarry waste the tramway's route is very clear and can be followed as it takes an initial north-westwards course and then curves eastwards. Just beyond the curve, pointwork indicates the direction of a loop-line to the left. The continuing line is carried over a wet area of former tin-workings on a slight embankment before being joined by the line coming from the other quarries to the west. This junction is marked by exceptionally well preserved pointwork, and by the use of smaller cut setts to effect the curve.

Here one may delay continuation eastwards along the main trunk in order to follow the tramway westwards (left) to the other four, smaller, quarries which it served. Along this stretch the route passes through a small cutting of heather-clad banks - the only one on the system. A little farther beyond, further pointwork marks access to a short length of line on the north side which was probably a siding or passing place. Shortly beyond this (SX 756777) is further pointwork where another northward branch takes off and descends half a mile to Holwell Quarry, with granite setts continuing to be well preserved. On the grass to the left, a little way down the track, at SX 755777, an unfinished cider pound base lies abandoned. In the approach to Holwell Quarry and within its area there is evidence of further

Track to Holwell Quarry

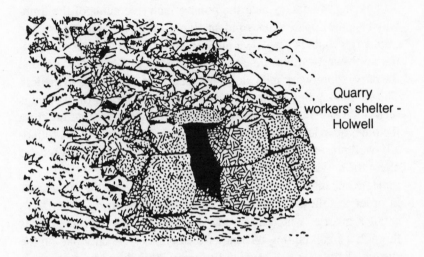

Quarry
workers' shelter -
Holwell

pointwork, sidings and switch-lines, and of substantial waste tips. The quarry has an impressive face and much fine granite was extracted from it. Building remains include a likely open-fronted store (SX 75137775) built against the edge of the quarry, which has a large cut boulder in its structure, and a small shelter shed built into the hillside, incorporating a natural rock, at SX 75197773. There is also an interesting beehive-shaped hut (SX 75107777) which was undoubtedly a workmen's shelter. Built of quarry waste, capped with large granite slabs and topped with stones, earth and heather, it was repaired by Dartmoor National Park Authority in 1987. Returning from Holwell Quarry to the main tramway one becomes aware of the gradient on this branch stretch. The rise, from 1100ft altitude to 1257ft, was the only length on the system on which the loaded waggons had to be hauled in ascent.

From the junction the westward exploration of the main tramway can be resumed. About ¹/₄ mile farther along a branch leaves on the left (south) side for the aptly named Rubble Heap Quarry (SX 755772), which is approached by a straight length of track bounded by tips of waste (apparently dumped here from the main Haytor Quarry), and curves to the east to enter a wide working area surrounded by rounded quarry faces.

Rejoining and continuing west along the main tramway, within a

very short distance the line is seen to divide. The two sections lead
off to serve respectively small quarries at either end of a distant long
rocky outcrop. This outcrop has no official map name, but has been
termed Emsworthy Rocks. Beyond this junction the 'rails' are far
less apparent, but the general direction is discernible in places, due to
the graded level and the occasional occurrence of granite setts, although much of the actual route has to be assumed. The right-hand
(north) fork may be followed initially. Along this line, near a bend, at
SX 75157723, are building remains - possibly those of stables. This
line served the workings at the extreme western end of the rocks (SX
748769) where there were two working faces, one on the north side
and the other around to the west. Several granite setts may be seen
within the area. Near the rocks, on the west side, are the remains of a
small circular beehive-shaped structure (SX 74897703) which was
probably a shelter for workers. Coming east, still north of the rocks,
are more prominent signs of buildings (SX 751769) in the form of a
rectangle of tumbled walling, with some sub-divisions, comprising
remains of former housing for the quarrymen. Just beyond this is the
eastern, or Harrow Barrow Quarry. This had three faces, including
one at the slightly higher level approached by a track around and up
to the east side. There is much evidence of the tramway within this
area including switch-stones for the different workings. The route of

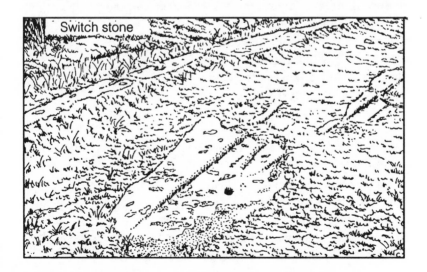

Switch stone

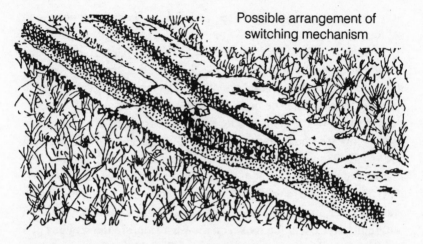

Possible arrangement of switching mechanism

the branch north, back towards the main tramway, can be assumed from the mainly straight course and slight ridge, and the triangular 'circuit' walked will be completed with the return to the earlier junction point.

The next stage will for some way be a retracing eastwards of the walk along the main trunk, passing the branch lines to Rubble Heap Quarry now on the right, to Holwell Quarry on the left, and eventually coming to the one to the main quarry on the right. The continuation on the main tramway is along a stretch which is particularly well preserved. About 300yds up the hillside, north of the tramway, just south of a grassy track alongside a reave, at SX 76457795 is a cut and shaped stone with a curved top. Now standing slightly askew and evidently used as a rubbing post for stock and as a perch for birds, it bears the letter T on one side and S on the other - undoubtedly for Templer and Somerset respectively.

T/S stone

At the crossing point of the Haytor Vale - Manaton road there has been some alteration and removal of the tramway setts which would have been about a foot higher than the present

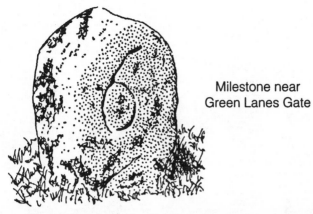

Milestone near
Green Lanes Gate

road. Just east of the road are signs of a further siding, on the north side. The route of the tramway continues, in gradual descent, coming close to the Bovey Tracey road and slightly above it. Signs of setts here are few and far between, but before the route leaves the Down the well-preserved 6 milestone is seen in situ on the left, at SX 779773. Swinging around northwards the tramway follows briefly the eastern extremity of the Down, and on reaching a further small disused quarry leaves the moorland and passes into the 'in-country'. This point also marks the end of the section of the tramway which is scheduled as an Ancient Monument by which it is the subject of statutory protection.

The six-mile route of the Haytor Granite Tramway from the 6 milestone and the boundary of Haytor Down to its meeting point with the Stover Canal is less continuously apparent than the stretches already covered, and lies in countryside of a different nature. Although some lengths still retain granite setts clearly in position many setts have been removed, and later developments have caused much obliteration. Some of the route lies within grounds that are now private and inaccessible. Nevertheless, much of the tramway can be followed, and where this is not possible acceptable deviations have been prescribed in a route authorised by co-operation between Dartmoor National Park, Teignbridge District Council, and Devon County Council, and called the Templer Way.

Immediately on leaving the Down the tramway route becomes inaccessible where it passes through farm land (the setts have been removed), and in order to rejoin it one must continue along the Bovey

Yarner Wood

road a short way and, from an acute left-hand junction, walk a short distance along the private road to Yarner. A sign shows where the route leads off from this road to the right, through Yarner Wood, which is a National Nature Reserve. This is a most delightful section for walkers, especially in the spring when the beech trees are coming into pale green leaf, and it provides many splendid viewpoints. By following the direction posts the course of the tramway is rejoined, and it becomes clearly visible. It is particularly impressive where it rounds the hillside on a right-handed curve, near which the 5 mile-stone stands on the bank on the right-hand side.

Soon after the milestone the route leaves the wood at a kissing gate and emerges on to Lower Down (SX 787785). The tramway can be followed fairly clearly around the contour, close above a wire fence amongst numerous gorse bushes. This is another scenic stretch with fine views to the north and east. On reaching another kissing gate the tramway route must again be left, as it proceeds through private ground. A rather muddy bridleway can be taken for the half mile back to the road at a point near Bracken Hill.

Continuing along the road towards Bovey Tracey, the tramway route is contacted again at Lowerdown Cross (SX 799781). Here one should diverge from the Bovey Tracey road and take Chapple Road (across to the right). The tramway route, having crossed over, runs within the private wood on the right-hand side of the road and roughly parallel to it, along a well-defined stretch where, in fact, the 4 mile-stone is located, on the left of the track. At the end of the wood the tramway route passes out of the enclosure at a gate (SX 802778) from where the setts continue along the descent on the west side of the road, sometimes at a higher level on the verge. An interesting point is then reached at Chapple Bridge where the tramway crosses the Pottery Leat carried on a small bridge - the only surviving one on the entire route. The cut rails are plainly seen on the approach and on the bridge itself. Having crossed the stream the tramway continues for a short distance on the west side of the road, behind the hedgebank, before it crosses the road from where its route forms a bridleway.

There is continued evidence of the tramway's setts along this bri-dle-way, although much of the granite has been obliterated. The route

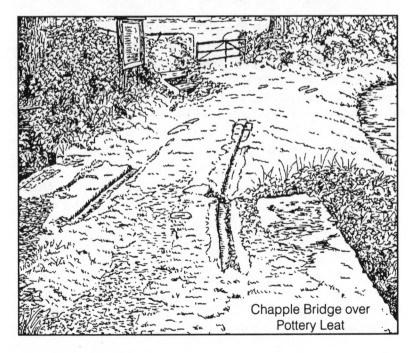

Chapple Bridge over
Pottery Leat

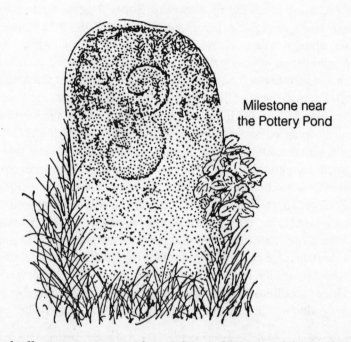

Milestone near
the Pottery Pond

gradually comes nearer to the southern urban area of Bovey Tracey, crossing first the road to Brimley and then the road from Bovey to Coldeast Cross. It then passes alongside gardens behind a row of houses, where the 3 milestone is preserved on the left, shortly before the Pottery Pond is seen, also on the left. From this point, at the junction with Pottery Road, the signs of the tramway are totally obliterated, due to industrial developments and the railway construction. Originally the tramway continued on a line south of the Pottery and across the main Newton Abbot-Bovey Tracey road (A 382). Near this point it was carried across a gully on a wooden bridge, where the waggons travelled on the only iron rails in the system. These are said to have been very similar to the type of iron rails cast at Coalbrookdale.

Since there is no public access from here for the remainder of the actual tramway's course, an alternative walking route is suggested as part of the Templer Way. This uses a line parallel to the tramway but about a mile west, running between Pottery Road and Great Plantation, originally planted by George Templer but now owned by the Forestry Commission. Crossing of the main dual carriageway A 38 road at Drum-bridges roundabout is necessary before the trail enters Stover Country Park, which occupies much of the parkland of Stover House, home of the Templers and now a girls' school. Information boards give details of walks within the Country Park, which is also noted for its wildlife, with two main alternative routes leading towards the River Teign.

The almost entire obliteration of this last stretch of the granite tramway, from Bovey's Pottery Road, was due to the construction of the Moretonhampstead and South Devon Railway, which followed the same route. In the approach to Ventiford, however, at Summerlane Bridge, the railway followed a straighter course, on a wide embankment, crossing twice the tramway route which here had meandered so as to lose height in order to reach the canal on a similar level. At Ventiford the railway passed between the canal and the tramway's route, with a bridge over a farm track. Former tramway rails were used here in the reconstruction and some can be clearly seen capping the wall between the track and the east-flowing Ventiford Brook. The house here at Ventiford was formerly an inn and also a smithy where, it is believed horses used on the tramway were shod.

Ventiford

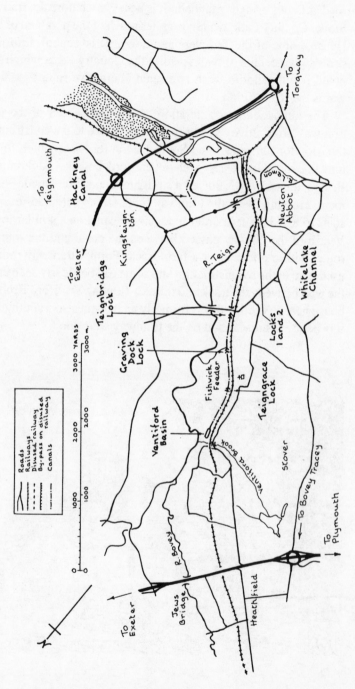

Stover Canal

THE STOVER CANAL

The area of the Stover Canal basin and wharf at Ventiford - the canal's upper terminus, 1 $^7/_8$ miles from its junction with the River Teign - is reached from the minor road north of Teigngrace, at Leygreen. It can be approached by way of the short track which passes beneath the railway bridge at SX 847748. The track is adjacent to the Ventiford Brook which was joined here by the canal's feeder from Jewsbridge. That feeder is now dry but part of its course can be seen to the north, adjacent to Summer Lane. A small weir may be seen in the brook, opposite a field gate, from where a sluice directed water into a culvert (now blocked) beneath the track to the canal basin on the south side. The filled-in canal basin is seen now as a depression in the rough grassy area, bounded by the remains of granite walls, curved at the basin's head. To gain an impression of the area in the time when the tramway was being worked and linked with the canal one should try and imagine the scene without the railway on its embankment. The wharf would then have extended on the west side from the basin to the road, and also on the east. Templer built clay cellars here in the 1790s, but these have long been demolished, although slight platforms have been identified on the east side as marking their sites. Two rectangular buildings on the west side, which have granite in their structure, were probably used for storing other goods, possibly including iron ore which was mined on the moor and transported via these quays. (Buildings just to the north by the Leygreen junction with Summer Lane, comprised a former pound house, timber yard and workshops).

The granite tramway terminated on the west bank quay, where it was totally obliterated by the railway embankment, although for a period there may also have been a tramway branch on the east quay. The granite blocks are believed to have been hoisted directly from the waggons into the boats by means of a crane, whose base is now concealed beneath an overgrown mound between the railway and the basin. The towpath was on the left-hand (east) side of the canal throughout. A short distance beyond the basin along the canal's route an arched culvert passes beneath the former waterway.

From Ventiford the Templer Way follows a brief diversion away from the canal along the banks of the River Teign, but the canal's next point of interest, half a mile south at Teigngrace village, can be reached also by road. A footpath leaving the road as it approaches a sharp bend leads to Locksbridge, involving a crossing of the railway line and then of the canal by means of the structure of the lock. This, the Teigngrace Lock (SX 849741) is well preserved, with ample evidence of the sturdy granite construction of its walls and floor. The stonework is of particularly fine finish in the vicinity of the lock gates. Of the gates the lower ones are non-existent, but at the upper end there are still rotting gate remains and those of its balance beam. The overgrown depression of the canal here nearly always contains some water. In the pre-railway days there was a dock and yard for boat building on the canal's west side. Barge building and repair work continued here in later years, despite developments at Graving Dock Lock (the next along the route) in the 1860s. The buildings at Locksbridge relate to that activity.

Below Locksbridge the course of the canal, generally overgrown, can be followed along the towpath. In about an eighth of a mile Grav-

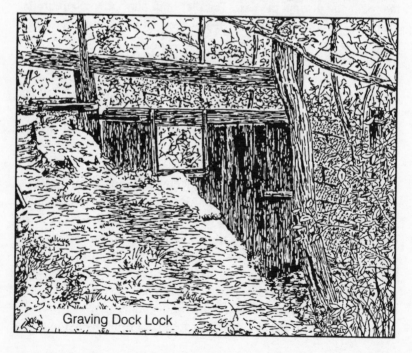

Graving Dock Lock

ing Dock Lock is reached (SX 853738). This lock is, of all, the best preserved, this being the highest point to which the canal was kept open after 1870, with the lock remaining in use until 1939. The still existing, but rotting, gates are probably replacements from the early 1900s. The lock is well-built of cut granite, curved on the east side where it was enlarged in the 1860s to form a new dry dock. A small brick building close by comprised a furnace where steaming of timbers for barge repairs and probably other processes were carried out.

Just south of Graving Dock Lock a small recess is seen on the canal's left (east) bank, and within a further short distance the canal is joined on the same bank by the Fishwick Feeder - the channel carrying water from the River Teign. This supplemented the supply of water to the canal and was not fully stopped off. Consequently the length of canal from here to the next lock normally contains water, providing a most attractive stretch and a habitat for wildlife.

Less than half a mile from Graving Dock Lock the canal reaches Teignbridge, where, at SX 856733, it passed by a bridge underneath the busy road. The lock here, just above the bridge, was of earthen

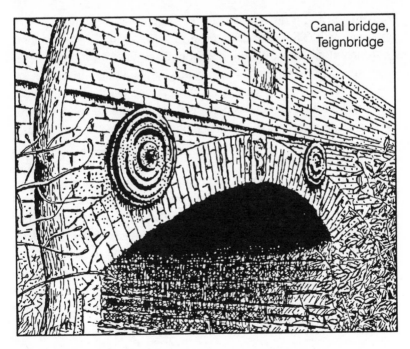

Canal bridge, Teignbridge

Keystone, Teignbridge
- south face

construction and little of it can now be seen due to infilling and veg-
etative growth. The canal bridge itself is of interest. Single-span, of
brick and stone construction, it was built in 1798. A tablet on the
north face gives the names of county magistrates at that time, with an
emblem of a goat's head on the arch keystone, while on the south
face keystone a man's head is portrayed. Level with the lock, west of
the canal, are stone stable buildings, now part of a scrapyard. South
of the bridge, on the east side of the canal are substantial long low
stone buildings which were originally clay cellars, used for storing
extracted clay, but which now form part of a vehicle repair and scrap
business. In all, twelve cellars were built here at the time of the canal's construction and in the following few years, contained within
two or three main sub-divided buildings. In modern times there has
been some demolition, and also rebuilding, but the main length of
the block remains. The cellars had double doorways, set opposite
each other, on the east and on the west (canal) side. In alterations
walls have been raised for greater roof space, and the heights of doors
correspondingly increased.

It is not possible to follow the course of the canal for the next stage due to latter-day clay workings, but it can be rejoined again on the edge of Newton Abbot, at Jetty Marsh Quay. This may be reached from the Newton Abbot-Kingsteignton road (A 380) just past the first roundabout near the DIY supercentre, where a turning into Jetty Marsh Lane on the north side of the road leads towards various industrial premises. A long building with low-pitch slightly undulating roof was originally a warehouse for coal and clay. This was generally a busy scene, with other industrial buildings and further clay cellars fronting on to the Whitelake Channel, a channel cut originally for draining the marsh but then used for importing and exporting goods for Newton Abbot, and for floating clay barges out on to the River Teign. Although there is limited public access on this bank of the Whitelake it may be possible to look across the channel and see the entrance lock of the Stover Canal. In any case this can be reached by returning to the main road, crossing the bridge over the Whitelake and entering on to a public footpath on the left. This leads to the canal's double locks and quay, (SX 861721). There were two lock

Mooring Post

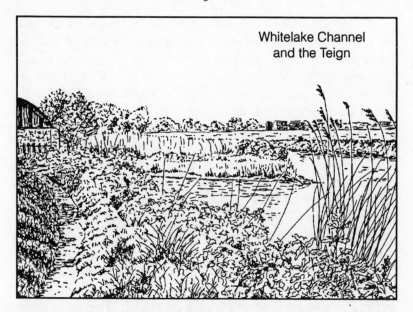

Whitelake Channel and the Teign

chambers, with three pairs of gates, and the basin between. On the outside of the lower gate's structure is a stone bearing the inscription: George Templer Esqr 1824, which probably relates to some rebuilding using dressed granite after construction of the tramway. Replacement of the lock's original earth structure with wood and masonry would have constituted further major improvements, which may also have been done at this time, or it could be that it was those that are commemorated by a further plaque on the basin's inner west wall inscribed: Duke of Somerset 1841. Along the quay are some iron mooring posts and beyond the lock a weir enabled the discharge of waste water. Whilst the lower lock remains in reasonable condition, the upper one, which was bridged by the railway, is completely obscured by a culvert and there are no signs of its two sets of gates.

In the canal's working days boats from the canal basin would pass out to the Whitelake Channel at high tide and travel the quarter-mile down to the River Teign. This route may be followed by again returning to the A380 road, crossing the bridge and the road, and entering a gate on the channel's west bank. From here there is an easy walk along a footpath which is crossed finally by the railway as the confluence is reached.

The Estuary of the Teign

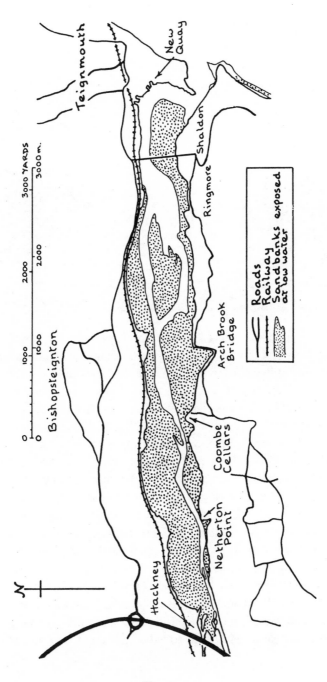

THE HACKNEY CANAL

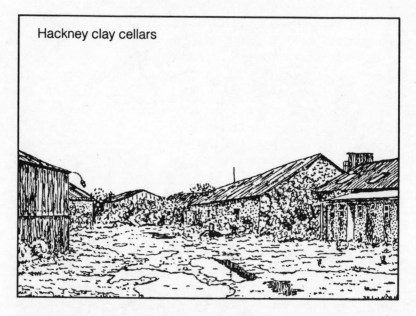

Hackney clay cellars

Although unconnected with the inland system of the Haytor Granite Tramway and the Stover Canal, a near neighbour, the Hackney Canal, shared the next stage of the waterway - the River Teign to the port of Teignmouth. The Hackney Canal's remains are but a short distance from those of the Stover Canal at Newton Abbot.

By proceeding eastwards on the A 380 road towards Kingsteignton, passing the racecourse, the site of the former canal basin with its remaining clay cellars is seen on the right, now the premises of a motor repair business (SX 869726). Just back from the road the two sets of former clay cellars extend south-eastwards. The space between them, now filled and levelled, was the canal basin, which broadened towards the road and extended by a slip-way close to the road itself. The northern group of buildings consists of three separate ones, comprising five former cellars. On the south side there are four buildings, providing seven. The buildings vary in date, the earliest - those built of rubble stone with dressed limestone quoins - probably originate from years immediately following the canal's opening in 1843. Others appear to have been added at times up to the turn of the century. The later cellars are of brick. Most have sets of central doors in oposite walls - single against the basin and double at the rear - similar to the arrangement at Teignbridge. Some buildings have been raised in height, and additional structures have been added.

Beyond the basin, where the canal was originally watered by the Ryder feeder coming from Kingsteignton, the $^5/_8$ mile route of the Hackney Canal is almost entirely filled in. Setting off south-eastwards it then turns slightly right to a more southerly direction in which it passes through what is now the racecourse. Its direction can mainly be assessed by taking a footpath which leads off the road north of the clay cellars. As it approaches the perimeter of the racecourse the canal route curves again towards the east before entering the lock (SX 873722) by which it connected with the River Teign. Built of granite, the lock, which held two barges in tandem, provided a rise of just over 3 $^1/_2$ ft. Only the ends of the lock are visible, a barrier and a sluice having been built into the centre to prevent flooding inland. No gates can be seen. The lock actually connects with a backwater of the Hackney channel of the Teign's old course.

The footpath continues alongside the channel eastwards to the earlier-worked area of Hackney Quay. On the north side of the path are various quay buildings consisting of probable boatmen's dwellings, stables, and possible stores for clay. Beyond these the path widens out into the present parking area by the Passage House Inn (which may also be approached by the signposted road). Here, on the site of the inn and the nearby conference centre, there were clay cellars, with a small dock adjoining (SX 879723). Hackney Quay was particularly busy in the eighteenth century, before construction of the Stover and Hackney Canals, when clay from the Kingsteignton area was dispatched from this point.

THE RIVER TEIGN

The last stage for the clay and granite traffic on its way to the export point at Teignmouth - the River Teign - can be conveniently followed on foot by proceeding down the right (west) bank of the estuary. Public footpaths follow the route as part of the Templer Way, continuing from the point, already described, where the Whitelake Channel joins the Teign. At low tide it may be possible to call to mind the dredging that was necessary in the nineteenth century, or when the tide is full to imagine the strange square-rigged barges plying their way downstream from one or other of the canals to off-load their cargoes.

On reaching Shaldon the continuation to Teignmouth can be made by crossing Shaldon Bridge - the modernised structure of the original bridge built in 1826-7, which incorporated a drawbridge for high vessels. The journey ends in Teignmouth's small docks area, at New Quay (SX 938727), built by George Templer in 1821 to enable the canal boats to transfer their cargoes to the 300 ton coastal vessels. The 3ft square, 1ft thick granite blocks of its construction are still prominent, steadfastly standing up to the pressures of wear and tear and thus displaying the high qualities of the rock of Haytor from whence they came.

The tug "Heron" towing barges

Bibliography

Since the 1960s M.C.Ewans' *The Haytor Granite Tramway and Stover Canal* (first published 1964) has been the standard work on the subject. It has now long been out of print, and virtually unobtainable. Ewans' book has provided the basis for this particular study, with much of his valuable material retained, and this is gratefully acknowledged. In addition there has been full updating to take into account changes on the ground, further research, and modern developments. Other sources of reference include:-

Amery Adams, W. 1946. 'The Old Haytor Granite Railway' *Transactions of the Devonshire Association 78.*

Hadfield, Charles. 1967. *The Canals of South West England* David & Charles.

Somers Cocks, J. 'The Haytor Granite Quarries' *Devon & Cornwall Notes and Queries 32.*

Harris, Helen. *The Industrial Archaeology of Dartmoor* (First pub. 1968, fourth [revised] edition Peninsula Press1992.)

Hemery, Eric. *Walking the Dartmoor Railroads* (First pub.1983, revised edition Peninsula Press 1991.)

Hemery, Eric. *Walking the Dartmoor Waterways* (First pub.1986, revised edition Peninsula Press 1991.)

Amenities and Countryside Division, Properties Department, Devon County Council; Dartmoor National Park Authority; Planning Department Teignbridge District Council.1985. *The Haytor Granite Tramway and Stover Canal, a Countryside Study.*

Dartmoor National Park Authority. 1987. *Archaeological survey of the Haytor Granite Tramway.*

Pye, A.R.1991. *An archaeological assessment of the Stover and Hackney Canals and Hackney Quay* (Exeter Museums Archaeological Field Unit).

Wade, P. *et al.*1990. *The Hackney Canal* A presentation by Coombeshead School.

Index

Acknowledgements

The author gratefully acknowledges assistance received from: Devon County Council Sites and Monuments Register; Dartmoor National Park Authority; Teignbridge District Council; information from Mr R.Wills, Dr Mary Freeman, Mr J.V. Somers Cocks; and firms who have kindly allowed access to their premises for viewing.

Illustrations

George Thurlow: pages 3, 4, 8-9, 12, 15, 17, 19, 23, 29, 30, 39, 40, 41, 42, 43, 44, 45, 46, 47, 48, 49, 50, 52, 53, 54, 55, 56, 57, 58, 60.
John Head (by kind permission of Dartmoor National Park Authority): front cover, pages 24, 25.

Peninsula Press

If you have enjoyed reading this book, and would like to receive a complete stock list of Peninsula Press titles, please send s.a.e. to:

Peninsula Press Limited
P.O. Box 31
Newton Abbot
Devon TQ12 5XH
Tel & Fax: 0803 875875